INTRODUCTION

Welcome to the Imperial War Museum. It is an unusual place in many ways – a museum devoted to modern war housed in an ancient lunatic asylum, it appears full of contradictions. The collections range from tanks and guns to works of art and films, yet our real subject is human behaviour. We deal with controversial and often unpleasant topics, but we also reflect the exceptional qualities of courage and self-sacrifice that are brought out

Dr Alan Borg CBE FSA, Director-General of the Imperial War Museum.

by war. At the same time we are as interested in the conscientious objector as we are in the military hero and we tell the story of the home front along with that of the front line.

This diversity of interest and the all-embracing nature of modern war make us perhaps the most comprehensive museum of the 20th century in existence. There is no one alive today whose life has not been shaped in some way by the great conflicts of this century and if that is a sad comment on humanity it also suggests that our subject is one that deserves study. The prime role of the Museum is educational, but we also know that you cannot educate anyone

if you are dull and boring. For this reason we have tried to make the new Imperial War Museum as lively and informative as possible. Our job is to tell you the facts in as accurate and objective a way as possible; the conclusions you draw are your own.

As in most museums, what you see on display is no more than the tip of the iceberg. We are in fact as much an archive as a museum, and the Reference Departments hold very large collections of material, all of which are available for study and research. We also have three other sites open to the public: HMS *Belfast*, the Cabinet War Rooms, and Duxford. I hope you will visit them as well but this is our headquarters and it is here that we try and cover all aspects of our story. It is your story too, whatever your age, country, or creed. Learn from it.

CONTENTS

FLOOR PLAN

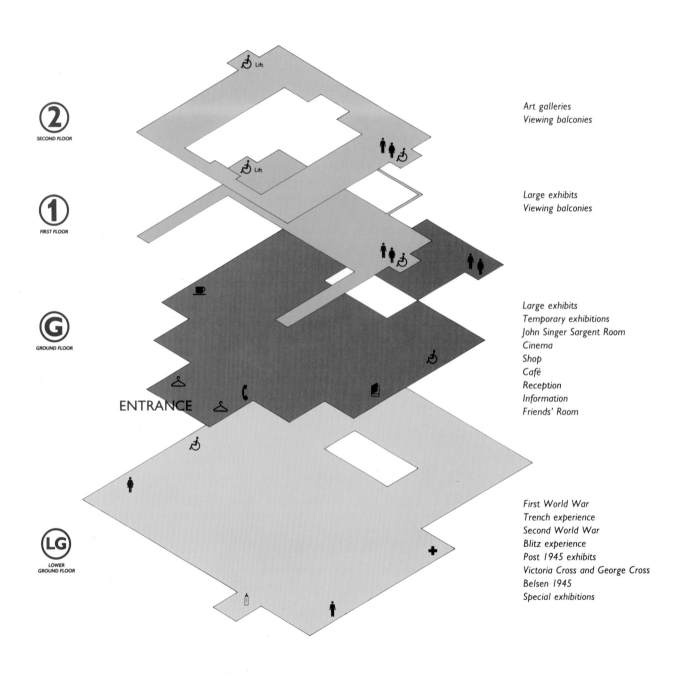

② SECOND FLOOR

Art galleries
Viewing balconies

① FIRST FLOOR

Large exhibits
Viewing balconies

Ⓖ GROUND FLOOR

Large exhibits
Temporary exhibitions
John Singer Sargent Room
Cinema
Shop
Café
Reception
Information
Friends' Room

ENTRANCE

ⓁⒼ LOWER GROUND FLOOR

First World War
Trench experience
Second World War
Blitz experience
Post 1945 exhibits
Victoria Cross and George Cross
Belsen 1945
Special exhibitions

KEY

 Lavatory

 First Aid room

 Shop

 Payphone

 Mother and baby room

☖ Cloakroom

 Café

♿ Lift Lift suitable for wheelchairs

LARGE EXHIBITS GALLERY

Views of the Large Exhibits Gallery.

The Large Exhibits Gallery, the impressive central space of Arup Associates' redevelopment of the original building, is the setting for some of the most important weapons and vehicles in the collections, including guns, tanks and aircraft.

MILITARY WEAPONS

Examples of several of the artillery pieces used in the world wars can be seen. Of special interest is a 13-pounder gun of E Battery, Royal Horse Artillery, which on 22 August 1914 fired the first British shell on land in the First World War. The 18-pounder was the standard British field gun and earned a reputation as one of the most reliable weapons of its type. Nearly 100 million rounds of 18-pounder ammunition were expended in France alone between 1914 and 1918, an average of 43 rounds for every minute of the war. The 75 mm, the French equivalent of the 18-pounder, was the first gun to be fitted with a recoil system and was renowned for its accuracy and rapidity of fire.

Heavy artillery includes a British 9.2-inch howitzer and a 60-pounder gun, which had a range of seven miles.

1   British 9.2-inch howitzer with a V1 directly above and a V2 to the left.

2   'J' Battery, Royal Horse Artillery, in open positions 1914. Q60751

3   British Mark IV tank in training, October 1917. Q6425

4   British Mark V tank. A Zeppelin gondola is shown above.

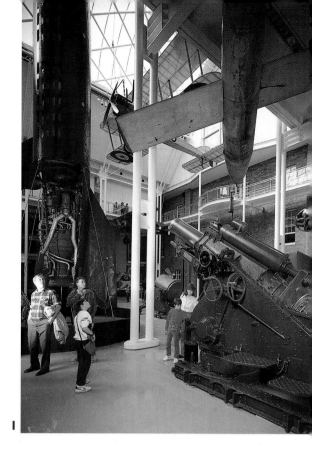

1

2

An example of one of the earliest mobile anti-aircraft guns is a 13-pounder mounted on a Thornycroft J-type lorry. Built in 1916, the lorry was restored to working order and took part in the 1987 London to Brighton commercial vehicle run. An unusual observation device is a German mast periscope designed for use behind buildings and in woods.

The tank – a British invention – was developed to break the deadlock of trench warfare. The Mark V represented an important advance in tank design. Introduced in 1918, it carried a crew of eight and could travel at a speed of 4½ miles an hour.

3

4

The earliest of the five Second World War tanks in the gallery is the British Infantry Mark II 'Matilda', a type which gave a good account of itself in France in 1940 and against the Italians in the Western Desert in the winter of 1940–1941. The German 8.8 cm was the only anti-tank gun able to penetrate its thick armour plating. The arrival of the M3 Grant in the Western Desert in the summer of 1942 at last gave the hard-pressed British Eighth Army a tank which could match the Panzer Mark IIIs and IVs of the German Afrika Korps. The slow but heavily armoured Churchill was one of the more successful British tanks and saw service in Tunisia, Italy and North West Europe. The principal armoured weapon of the Allied armies was the American-built M4 Sherman, which was produced in greater numbers than any other tank. The Russian T-34 combined speed with endurance and was perhaps the outstanding tank of the war, playing a decisive role in the great armoured battles on the Eastern Front.

The two remaining Second World War military vehicles are a Daimler armoured car and the ubiquitous jeep, of which more than 600,000 were built.

Anti-tank weapons include the formidable Jagdpanther, an 8.8 cm self-propelled gun; a 17-pounder, the most powerful British anti-tank gun; and a German 5 cm Pak.

The 5.5-inch gun was the standard equipment of British medium artillery regiments and served in all the major theatres from 1942. The Nebelwerfer projectile launcher was employed by the Germans in considerable numbers in the later stages of the war and the terrifying scream of its rockets was a familiar sound to Allied troops in Normandy in 1944. A 4.7 ton shell from a massive German 80 cm gun is displayed. Nicknamed *Schwerer Gustav* ('Heavy Gustav'), it was the largest gun ever built but fired only 48 rounds during the war – against Sebastopol in 1942.

2

3

4

1   *Grant tanks lined up in the Western Desert, 17 February 1942.* E8487

2   *M4 Sherman tank.*

3   *Jagdpanther tank destroyer.*

4   *A Daimler armoured car engaging enemy targets during the battle for Tripoli, 18 January 1943.* E21333

NAVAL WEAPONS

The first British shot in the First World War was fired by a 4-inch gun from the destroyer HMS *Lance*. Another naval exhibit of note is the 5.5-inch gun from HMS *Chester* which the sixteen-year-old Boy First Class Jack Cornwell was serving when he was mortally wounded at the Battle of Jutland. He was posthumously awarded the Victoria Cross.

The use of submarines presented a new threat both to warships and to merchant shipping, as we are reminded by a 10.5 cm gun from U98.

An unusual example of a Second World War submarine is the German one-man Biber, which was hastily developed for operations against the Allied invasion flotilla in 1944. Another specialised underwater craft is the Italian 'human torpedo', which was employed with spectacular success against the British battleships *Queen Elizabeth* and *Valiant* in Alexandria harbour towards the end of 1941. The *Tamzine* is the smallest surviving fishing boat to have taken part in Operation 'Dynamo', the evacuation of British and French troops from Dunkirk in 1940.

1   *A U-boat fires her deck gun during a training exercise in the Baltic. 1917.* Q53038

2   *German one-man Biber submarine.*

3   *The fishing boat* Tamzine.

1

2

3

AIR WEAPONS

The military possibilities of aircraft were not fully appreciated in 1914 but by the end of the war they had begun to exert a significant influence on the conduct of land operations. Two First World War aircraft are displayed, an early two-seat reconnaissance machine – the BE2c – and a Sopwith Camel 2F1, the naval version of the celebrated British fighter. Also on view is the observation car from a Zeppelin (probably LZ90), which was found near Colchester after an air raid in 1916.

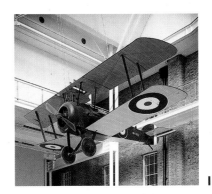

1

1   *Sopwith Camel 2F1.*
This particular aircraft was flown by Lieutenant S D Culley when he shot down the German Zeppelin L53 over the North Sea in 1918.

2   *Royal Aircraft Factory BE2c.*

3   *This BE2A, photographed near Whitby in August 1914, was the first British aircraft to land in France after the outbreak of the First World War. The pilot, Lieutenant H D Harvey-Kelly, is relaxing at the foot of the haystack.*
Q54985

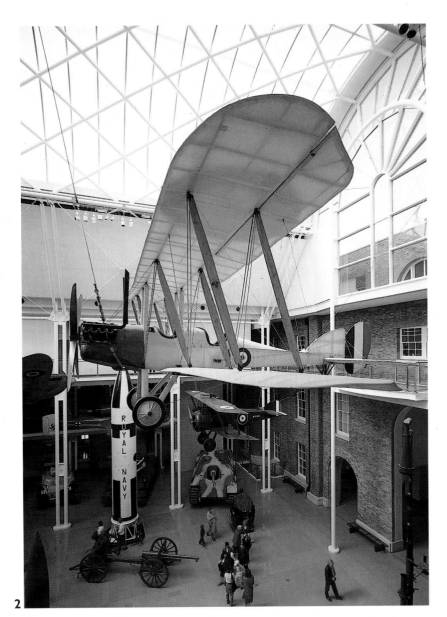

2

3

The Museum is fortunate to have in its collection of Second World War aircraft a Supermarine Spitfire Mark 1A which saw action in the Battle of Britain. Another exceptional Allied fighter was the North American P-51 Mustang. With auxiliary fuel tanks it was capable of escorting the bombers of the United States Eighth Air Force to Berlin and back, and it made a crucial contribution to the battle for air supremacy over Germany. German Second World War aircraft consist of a Focke Wulf 190 and a Heinkel 162. The radial-engined FW190, which the RAF first encountered in 1941, was one of the fastest and most manoeuvrable fighters of the war. The He162 'Salamander' jet fighter was rushed into production at the end of 1944 in a vain attempt to combat the growing power of the Allied air offensive.

The German *Vergeltungswaffen* (reprisal weapons), the V1 and V2, were launched against England in the second half of 1944. The V1, known as the 'doodlebug' or 'buzz bomb', was a

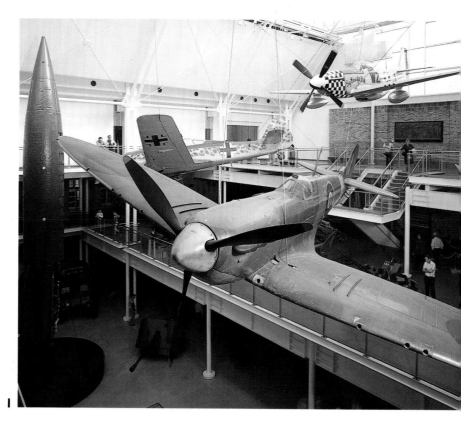

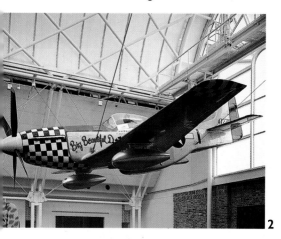

1   Battle of Britain Spitfire.

2   North American P-51 Mustang.

3   Lieutenant-Colonel J D Landers, commander of the 78th Fighter Group at Duxford, with his P-51D Mustang, 'Big Beautiful Doll', on 24 March 1945. The Museum's Mustang has been painted to represent this aircraft. HU31358

jet-propelled pilotless aircraft with a speed of about 400 miles an hour. The V2 rocket, forerunner of today's missiles, travelled faster than sound and was impossible to intercept. A total of over 6,500 V weapons fell on London and the South East, killing 8,938 people.

The post-war Polaris was the first submarine-based ballistic missile and has carried Britain's independent nuclear deterrent since 1968.

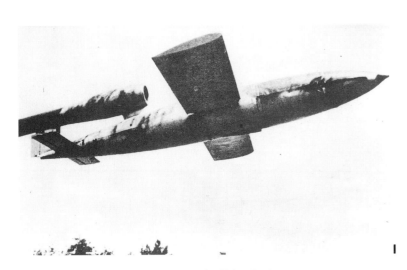

1   V1 *flying bomb.* CL.3433

2   *V2 rocket.*

3   *Polaris missile.*

4   *Polaris submarine.* CT105

FIRST FLOOR

The exhibits in this area chiefly relate to air warfare. They include a one-pounder anti-aircraft gun, which in September 1915 fired (unsuccessfully) at the first Zeppelin to raid the City of London; the cockpit sections of a Mitsubishi A6M Zero-Sen fighter – the Japanese equivalent of the Spitfire – and of an Avro Lancaster and a Handley Page Halifax, which together formed the backbone of the Royal Air Force's bombing offensive against Germany; a German 8.8 cm high velocity anti-aircraft gun which was also used, with devastating effect, in an anti-tank role; part of the fuselage and one of the Daimler-Benz engines from the Messerschmitt 110 in which Rudolf Hess flew to Scotland in May 1941; and German 'Small Würzburg' radar equipment.

Post-Second World War exhibits include a BAC Thunderbird 2, a surface to air guided missile designed to intercept fast high-flying aircraft; and a 20 mm twin-mounted anti-aircraft gun captured from the Argentinians during the Falklands War in 1982.

1   Fuselage section of a Lancaster bomber.

2   Cockpit section of a Japanese Zero fighter.

3   Thunderbird missile.

During
this century
more than
100,000,000
people have
died as a
result of
war.

THE FIRST WORLD WAR

THE ORIGINS AND OUTBREAK OF THE WAR

The causes of the First World War were complex and are the subject of continuing historical debate. The rise of Germany after 1871 upset the old balance of power in Europe. Tensions were heightened by conflicting national ambitions, economic competition and colonial rivalries. By 1914 an elaborate system of alliances divided Europe into two armed camps. Any incident involving one country threatened to start a chain reaction dragging them all into war. Such an incident occurred at Sarajevo on 28 June 1914 when the heir to the throne of Austria-Hungary, Archduke Franz Ferdinand, was assassinated.

By the end of July the armed forces of Europe were mobilising. Britain declared war on Germany on 4 August 1914, shortly after the Kaiser's armies had crossed the Belgian frontier. Britain was the only major European power without a conscript army. Field Marshal Lord Kitchener, Secretary of State for War, believed that the struggle would be long and costly. He at once set about creating volunteer 'New Armies'. By the end of 1915 nearly two and a half million men had enlisted. In 1916 Parliament passed Military Service Acts, which introduced the conscription of men between 18 and 41.

1

1   The famous Kitchener poster, designed by Alfred Leete.

2   The 16th (The Queen's) Lancers during the advance from the Marne to the Aisne, September 1914. Q56309

3   Parliamentary Recruiting Committee poster by E V Kealey.

3

THE WESTERN FRONT

The German bid to inflict a swift and decisive defeat on France was checked at the Battle of the Marne in September 1914. By then it had become clear that the range, accuracy and fire power of modern weapons, in particular the defensive capability of the machine gun, were such that soldiers could only survive on the battlefield by taking shelter in trenches. Attempts by each side to outflank the other failed and by December 1914 the opposing lines of trenches extended from the English Channel to the Swiss frontier. For four years the combatants sought ways of ending the stalemate of trench warfare. On a tactical level this resulted in successive attempts to breach the enemy trench lines by the use of massive artillery bombardments, the employment of gas and the development of the tank. Trench warfare created a world of its own – at worst a wilderness of shattered trees, barbed wire entanglements and waterlogged craters. Soldiers on both sides had to contend with difficulties of communication and supply, the misery of wet, cold, mud, rats and lice, and the strain of living under the ever-present threat of death or mutilation. The unprecedented number of casualties and the dreadful wounds caused by high-explosive shells stretched and challenged the medical services.

1   A Vickers machine gun near Ovillers on the Somme in July 1916. Q3995

2   Tank poster, c. 1917, by Charles Frederick Higham.

3   First World War trench equipment: a British Mills bomb, PH anti-gas helmet and trench club and a German stick grenade.

THE TRENCH

One of the principal features of the First World War exhibition is a walk-through re-creation of a front line trench on the Somme in the autumn of 1916. Visitors can experience at first hand what it was like to be a tommy in the trenches. The re-creation is brought to life with special lighting, sound and smell effects.

1

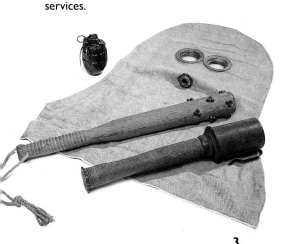

3

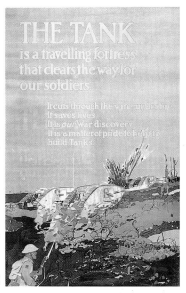

2

THE TANK is a travelling fortress that clears the way for our soldiers.

Third Ypres, 1917: Australian troops passing along a duckboard track through devastated Chateau Wood. E(1914)1220.

What passing-bells for these who die as cattle?
– Only the monstrous anger of the guns.
Only the stuttering rifles' rapid rattle
Can patter out their hasty orisons.

No mockeries now for them; no prayers nor bells;
Nor any voice of mourning save the choirs, –
The shrill, demented choirs of wailing shells;
And bugles calling for them from sad shires.

What candles may be held to speed them all?
Not in the hands of boys, but in their eyes
Shall shine the holy glimmers of goodbyes.
The pallor of girls' brows shall be their pall;
Their flowers the tenderness of patient minds,
And each slow dusk a drawing-down of blinds.

Anthem for Doomed Youth by Wilfred Owen

POETS AND PAINTERS

The horror of the Western Front inspired some memorable poetry. The major war poets – Edmund Blunden, Siegfried Sassoon, Robert Graves, Isaac Rosenberg and Wilfred Owen – all had first-hand experience of the trenches. Their poems, written in direct and sometimes brutal language, were a protest against what they saw as the tragic waste and futility of the conflict. The war also provided powerful subject matter for artists such as John and Paul Nash, C R W Nevinson, Stanley Spencer, William Roberts and Eric Kennington. From 1916 they and many others were employed as official war artists to record scenes on the home and fighting fronts.

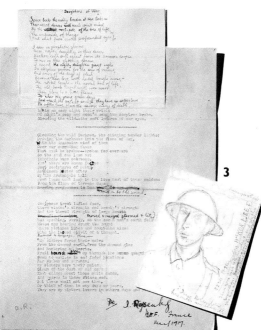

1 *Siegfried Sassoon.*
Copyright Radio Times Hulton Picture Library.

2 *Sketch for* Over the Top *by John Nash.*

3 *Manuscript by the war poet and artist Isaac Rosenberg.*

4 *Isaac Rosenberg.*
Q93488

WAR IN THE AIR

As trench warfare settled in on the Western Front, armies became dependent upon the aeroplane as a means of discovering what the enemy was doing. Decisive combats between aircraft were rare in the early months of the war but each side quickly saw the need to win dominance over the opposing air service. This led to the specialisation of aircraft types and hastened the development of the single-seat fighter. From 1916 the air war became a see-saw struggle for supremacy. New aircraft were introduced and tactics constantly refined and improved. By the middle of 1917 air combat had become a matter of team fighting rather than individual scouting. The best-known fighter formation was the 'Richthofen Circus', led by Baron Manfred von Richthofen, an astute tactician and deadly shot, whose distinctive red Albatros became the symbol of dominance over the Western Front. Other 'aces' included the British airmen Captain Albert Ball, Major 'Mick' Mannock and Major James McCudden, Lieutenant Colonel W A 'Billy' Bishop – a Canadian – and the French pilot Capitaine Georges Guynemer.

1

1 SE5 and SE5As of No. 29 Squadron, RAF, Oudezeele, August 1918. Q60608

2 Aerial photograph taken on 15 July 1915 during preparations for the Battle of Loos. Q60546

2

1 Second-Lieutenant Albert Ball,
a photograph probably taken
in 1915. Q69593

2 The Last Flight of Captain
Ball VC, DSO, MC, 7 May
1917 by Norman G Arnold.

3 Model of Fokker DrI triplane.

4 Baron Manfred von Richthofen
in the cockpit of his Albatros
DIII with pilots of his 'Flying
Circus'. Q42283

THE WAR ON OTHER FRONTS

The most important theatre of the war after France was the Eastern Front, where Germany and Austria-Hungary confronted Russia and Serbia. Much was expected of the Russian 'steamroller'. But by 1917 the Russian army had suffered enormous losses and, despite winning a notable victory against the Austrians in the summer of 1916, was exhausted and demoralised. The October Revolution ended the Russian war effort and on 3 March 1918 Russia and Germany signed a peace treaty at Brest Litovsk. In addition to the Eastern Front there were a number of 'side shows'. Well over a million British, Indian and Dominion troops took part in campaigns against Germany's ally,

1

2

Turkey – on the Gallipoli peninsula, and in Egypt, Palestine and Mesopotamia. In 1915 an Allied expeditionary force, which eventually grew to 600,000 men, was landed at Salonika to oppose the Bulgarians. French and British contingents were sent to support the Italians in November 1917 after an Austro-German army had inflicted a crushing defeat on them at Caporetto. Further afield, British and German forces fought a long-running campaign in East Africa.

3

1   *Anzac Beach, Gallipoli, 1915.* Q13603

2   *Short Magazine Lee-Enfield Mark III rifle used by T E Lawrence.* Q44270

3   *T E Lawrence in the desert, 1917.* Q59314

THE WAR AT SEA

Britain looked to the Royal Navy for protection against invasion and to keep the sea lanes open for essential supplies of food and raw materials. There were engagements between British warships and German commerce raiders in the Indian Ocean, the Pacific and the South Atlantic. The long-awaited clash between the British Grand Fleet and the German High Seas Fleet took place at Jutland on 31 May 1916. Although the battle was tactically indecisive the High Seas Fleet, apart from one or two abortive sorties, remained locked in its bases for the rest of the war. The British blockade of German ports caused great hardship in Germany. The Germans retaliated by mounting a submarine campaign against Allied merchant shipping. This brought Britain close to defeat but also precipitated America's entry into the war in April 1917. The adoption of the convoy system and a substantial increase in British and American shipbuilding enabled the Allies to overcome the U-boat menace.

1

3

2

1   *Ships of the Grand Fleet in line ahead, First World War.*
Q63698

2   *German U-boat poster ('The U-boats are out!') by H R Erdt.*

3   *Admiral Sir John Jellicoe on board HMS* Iron Duke.
Q55499

4   *Breeches buoy from the* Lusitania.

4

THE HOME FRONT

The First World War had an unprecedented effect on civilian life. Shortly after the outbreak of war the government brought in the Defence of the Realm Act, which gave it sweeping powers. News was censored, the coal mines nationalised, land and property requisitioned for military purposes, the sale of alcohol restricted and Summer Time introduced. Food rationing was instituted in 1918. Recruiting caused labour shortages which resulted in large numbers of women doing jobs in industry, transport, agriculture and commerce previously done by men. Some 100,000 women joined the newly formed auxiliary services of the three armed forces. Zeppelin and aircraft raids caused much dislocation and put civilians in the front line for the first time. The war also made its impact on an emotional level, with almost every family being affected by the death or wounding of a relative or friend.

1 Amputees convalescing at No.2 New Zealand General Hospital, Oatlands Park, Roehampton, 1917.

2 Recruiting poster for Queen Mary's Army Auxiliary Corps.

3 Chilwell Shell-Filling Factory, July 1917. Q30011

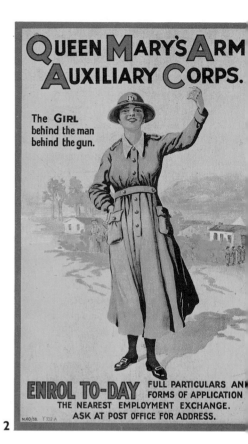

1 Bomb damage in London caused by a Zeppelin raid in October 1915. LCI

2 German incendiary bomb dropped by Zeppelin LZ38 on 31 May 1915 during the first airship raid on London.

3 First World War aircraft identification poster.

END OF THE WAR

Hostilities on the Western Front ceased at 11am on 11 November 1918 when an armistice between Germany and the Allies came into effect. A final settlement, determined by a peace conference, was embodied in the Treaty of Versailles, which was signed by the Germans, under protest, on 28 June 1919. Germany lost territory and its armed forces were greatly reduced. It had to pay massive compensation for war damage and admit its guilt for causing the war. These terms provoked great bitterness in Germany and sowed the seeds of future discord in Europe.

1   *Next of kin memorial plaque.*

2   *Grave of an unknown British soldier, Thiepval, September 1916. Q1540*

THE SECOND WORLD WAR

THE INTER-WAR YEARS

Hopes for a lasting peace after the
First World War were short-lived.
The next two decades witnessed a
series of wars and diplomatic crises
that pointed the way to a new global
conflict. Totalitarian states were
established in Italy after 1922 under
Benito Mussolini's Fascist party and in
Nazi Germany, where Adolf Hitler
became Chancellor in 1933. Germany
began to rearm and to create an air
force. In March 1936 Hitler
reoccupied the demilitarised
Rhineland and two years later
marched into Austria. Shortly

1

2

1 Nazi election poster.

2 Pottery head of Benito
   Mussolini by Bertelli.

3 Neville Chamberlain waving
   the text of his agreement with
   Hitler on his return from
   Munich, 30 September 1938.
   D2239

4 Models of Nazi standard
   bearers, made in Germany by
   Elastolin in the 1930s.

5 Nazi Party rally, Nuremberg,
   1934. NYP10979D

3

afterwards, at the Munich
Conference, he persuaded the
Western powers to force
Czechoslovakia to cede the
Sudetenland. In March 1939 Germany
occupied the rest of Czechoslovakia.
The German invasion of Poland on
1 September 1939 marked the end
of the policy of appeasement pursued
by the British prime minister, Neville
Chamberlain. Britain and France
declared war on Germany on
3 September, though they were
unable to intervene effectively on
Poland's behalf.

4

5

THE PHONEY WAR

Having failed to prevent the defeat of Poland, which was overwhelmed in a campaign lasting under three weeks, Britain and France were faced with the prospect of a long and costly war with Germany. Britain braced itself for an all-out German attack and civil defence plans were put into effect. Although there was some action at sea, there was little activity on land or in the air. The war developed a sense of unreality which earned it the title of the 'Phoney War'.

2

3

1 Baby's gas mask, a photograph taken shortly after the outbreak of war. HU36124

2 Enigma encyphering machine.

3 Schoolchildren being evacuated from London, September 1939. HU36238

4 A child's 'Mickey Mouse' gas mask (left) and the adult's version.

5 Blackout poster.

4

5

BLITZKRIEG

In the spring of 1940 Germany launched Blitzkrieg (lightning war) attacks in Scandinavia and Western Europe. German forces invaded Norway in April and the Low Countries and France on 10 May – the day on which Winston Churchill became prime minister. The main German attack was directed not against the heavily fortified Maginot Line but through the lightly defended Ardennes. German tanks and assault troops with close air support broke through the French line and drove

1

northwards towards the sea, splitting the Allied armies in two. The British Expeditionary Force and the French First Army were cornered at Dunkirk but 338,000 managed to escape, thanks to a hasty but effective evacuation operation mounted across the English Channel. The German advance against the bulk of the French forces continued until an armistice was agreed on 22 June.

1   *Junkers Ju87.* GER18

2   *Men of The Royal Ulster Rifles waiting to be evacuated from Dunkirk.* HU1135

2

THE BATTLE OF BRITAIN

After the collapse of France, Britain stood alone. In July 1940 Hitler directed that plans be drawn up for an invasion of the British mainland, codenamed Operation 'Sealion'. But before the invasion could be mounted the Germans had to win command of the skies over southern England by defeating the Royal Air Force. The Luftwaffe began its main offensive on 13 August 1940, attacking airfields, radar stations, ports and aircraft factories. Fighter Command was down to its last reserves when, on 7 September, the assault was unexpectedly switched to London. The Luftwaffe's efforts intensified but so did its losses. On 17 September Hitler postponed 'Sealion' indefinitely.

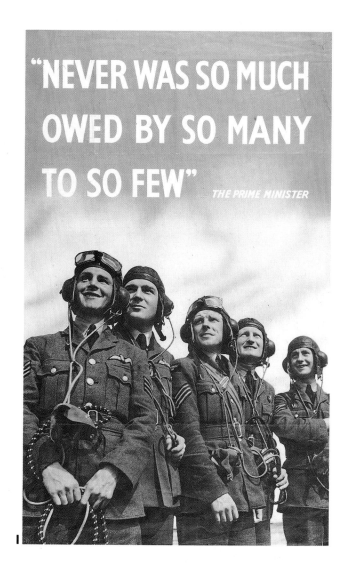

1

2

3

1 Battle of Britain poster.

2 Goering and his staff officers on the Channel coast, 1 July 1940. HU1185

3 'Careless talk' poster.

4 Spitfires on patrol. CH740

4

THE HOME FRONT

Unable to launch an invasion, Germany tried instead to bomb Britain into submission. The Blitz, the period of most sustained bombing, lasted from September 1940 until the late spring of 1941. London was attacked on fifty-seven consecutive nights and fifteen other British cities, notably Coventry, suffered extensive damage. Over 41,000 British civilians were killed and 137,000 injured. Britain came under

1 *ARP recruiting poster.*

2 *Fore Street in the City of London during the Blitz.*

3 *The Elephant and Castle underground station, 11 November 1940.* D1568

4 *Detail from 'Seeing it through' poster by Eric Kennington, 1944.*

2

heavy attack again in 1944 from Germany's secret weapons, the V1 and the V2. The country endured not only air raids but also severe shortages of food and raw materials. Life in Britain was hard and drab. Every kind of resource was mobilised for the war effort. The conscription of men and women into civil as well as military occupations was introduced: by the middle of 1944 over 460,000 women were in the services and six and a half million were engaged in civilian war work. Britain became home to thousands of refugees as well as foreign servicemen, especially Americans, once preparations began for an Allied invasion of Europe.

3

4

1   Utility symbol.

2   Examples of wartime food
     packaging and a Second
     World War ration book.

3   Industrial recruiting poster by
     Zec.

2

WOMEN OF BRITAIN
COME INTO
THE FACTORIES

ASK AT ANY EMPLOYMENT EXCHANGE FOR ADVICE AND FULL DETAILS

3

THE BLITZ EXPERIENCE

The Blitz Experience is a carefully researched reconstruction of an air-raid shelter and a blitzed street in 1940. Appropriate sights, sounds and smells evoke for visitors a sensation of being caught in the bombing of London during the Second World War.

4   One of the best-known Second
     World War posters.

DIG FOR VICTORY

4

THE WAR AT SEA AGAINST GERMANY AND ITALY

For Britain, dependent upon imports, command of the sea was vital. The German surface fleet, which included the battleships *Bismarck* and *Tirpitz* as well as other powerful modern warships, represented a constant menace to Allied merchant shipping; in the event it did relatively little damage. The flow of raw materials, food, munitions and men from North America was the key to Britain's survival. As in the First World War,

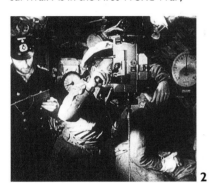

German submarines posed the biggest threat to the supply routes. The U-boats inflicted losses averaging 96 ships a month in 1942 but by the middle of 1943 the Battle of the Atlantic had swung in favour of the Allies. Better anti-submarine weapons and detection devices, trained convoy support groups, escort carriers and long-range aircraft all helped to defeat the U-boats. Shipping in the Mediterranean and convoys carrying Allied supplies to Russia were also at risk. Out of 40 Arctic convoys, 89 merchant ships and 18 warships were sunk.

1 HMS Scylla *during the passage of convoy JW53 to Russia in February 1943.* A15365

2 *A U-boat commander at the periscope sights.* FLM1460

3 *Model of a German Type VII U-boat.*

4 *The carriers* Indomitable *and* Eagle *off Malta during Operation 'Pedestal', August 1942.* A15961h

5 *Model of the battlecruiser HMS* Hood, *sunk in 1941.*

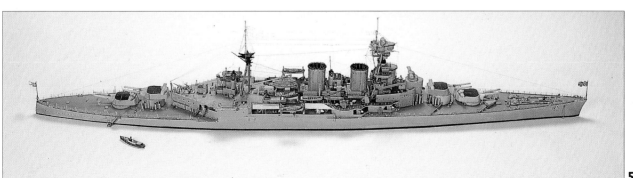

MEDITERRANEAN AND MIDDLE EAST

As Germany completed the domination of Western Europe, fighting began in the Mediterranean theatre. German forces swept through Greece in the spring of 1941 and in an airborne invasion of Crete forced British troops to evacuate the island. Earlier, an Italian attack on Egypt had been successfully repulsed but the German Afrika Corps, sent to reinforce the Italians early in 1941, posed a new threat in the Western Desert under the aggressive leadership of General Rommel. In June 1942 Rommel captured the important port of Tobruk. Two months later Lieutenant-General Montgomery took command of the British Eighth Army and ended its series of defeats by winning a decisive victory over the Axis forces at the Battle of El Alamein in November. Operation 'Torch', the landing of three British and American armies under the command of General Eisenhower, led in May 1943 to the surrender of the Axis forces in North Africa. The capture of Sicily in August 1943 and the subsequent invasion of Italy gave the Allies their first foothold on the European mainland since 1940. German forces seized control of Italy when the Italians agreed to an armistice with the Allies. The advance through Italy was slow and costly but by the spring of 1945 the Allies had reached the north Italian plains. The Germans surrendered unconditionally on 2 May.

1   Breaking through the last of the German minefields at El Alamein. *Alex Ingram.*

2   *General Montgomery in his Grant tank. This tank is displayed in the Large Exhibits Gallery.* E18980 (KT)

3   *Ukelele made at Tobruk in 1941.*

4   *German paratroopers fighting among the ruins of the monastery at Monte Cassino, April 1944.* MH6352

1

2

3

4

EASTERN FRONT

Strategic, economic and ideological motives lay behind Hitler's decision to order the invasion of Russia. The German offensive, Operation 'Barbarossa', began on 22 June 1941, taking the Soviet forces by surprise. Employing well-tried Blitzkrieg tactics, the three-million strong force struck deep into the Soviet heartland, capturing whole Russian armies before coming to a halt on the outskirts of Leningrad and Moscow. In December 1941 the Soviet Union surprised the Germans by mounting a counter-offensive, easing the pressure on Moscow. Hitler turned his attention to the south and attacked in the Caucasus in the spring of 1942. His armies were comprehensively defeated at Stalingrad early in 1943 and in the Battle of Kursk in the summer, which cost the Wehrmacht half a million men. The Germans, fighting doggedly, were steadily driven from Soviet territory.

1

3

2

1 *Russian patriotic poster.*

2 *Russian infantry advancing during the Soviet winter offensive of 1942.* RUS2109

3 *German straw 'snow' boots used on the Eastern Front.*

4 *German Panzer Mark III and assault troops, a photograph probably taken in the Ukraine in 1941.*

4

EUROPE UNDER THE NAZIS

In the wake of German victory came Nazi exploitation of the conquered territories. Occupied Europe's agricultural and industrial output was channelled to meet Germany's needs, regardless of the deprivation this caused to home markets. The Nazis imposed repressive racial and political policies. Although the severity of German rule varied greatly from country to country, no community remained untouched. The first attempts at resistance in Occupied Europe were largely isolated and ill-coordinated acts of personal opposition. But with the passage of time, men, women and children joined together to confront their oppressors. An alternative to Nazi propaganda was provided by the illegal press. Escape lines and intelligence networks helped the Allied war effort. Where circumstances permitted, resisters carried out a guerilla war against the German and collaborationist forces. However, effective armed resistance was largely dependent on support from one of the Allies' own clandestine organisations.

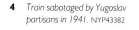

2

3

4

1 Members of the Dutch underground movement. BU2887

2 An example of a Red Cross parcel sent to British prisoners of war in Germany during the Second World War.

3 1943 pattern 'escape' boot, compass and silk map. These formed part of the escape and evasion equipment issued to RAF aircrew.

4 Train sabotaged by Yugoslav partisans in 1941. NYP43382

Buchenwald survivors. EA63141

CONCENTRATION CAMPS

Concentration camps were established in Germany shortly after Hitler's assumption of power in 1933. Many of the Nazis' political opponents were arrested. Socialists, communists, Jews, gipsies, vagabonds, homosexuals, pacifists, trade unionists and Jehovah's Witnesses were among those imprisoned. After the outbreak of war, new concentration camps were set up throughout Occupied Europe to deal with the millions of foreign opponents of German domination. Extermination camps were established to implement the 'Final Solution', the systematic killing of more than six million Jews.

THE BOMBER OFFENSIVE

The strategic air offensive played a major, but not decisive, role in the defeat of Germany by attacking the enemy's economic strength and will to resist. The ineffectiveness of operations up to the end of 1941 exposed the weakness of the RAF. Aircraft, bombs and navigational equipment were inadequate and losses in daylight raids caused Bomber Command to switch to night attacks. From February 1942 Air Marshal Harris adopted the 'area' bombing of German cities in an attempt to disrupt industrial production and morale. On 31 May 1942 the first 'thousand bomber' raid was launched against Cologne. In August 1942 the American Eighth Air Force joined the offensive and began precision daylight bombing against key targets. In 1943 and 1944 the RAF attacked the Ruhr, Hamburg and Berlin. Enemy fighters took a heavy toll and German war production actually increased until July 1944. The arrival of long-range escort fighters transformed the bomber offensive in the last phase of the war. The controversial area bombing policy culminated in the destruction of Dresden in February 1945, causing thousands of civilian deaths. The bomber offensive was extremely costly, with Bomber Command losing 55,573 aircrew and 1,570 ground staff.

1   *Lancasters of RAF Bomber Command attacking Bremen, 21 March 1945.* C5101

2   *Wing-Commander Guy Gibson, VC.* MH6673

3   *Part of the briefing model for the Dams Raid.*

1 American B-17 Flying
  Fortresses. HU4052

2 USAAF leather flying jacket.

3 Dresden, photographed a few
  years after the war. HU3321

4 Members of the German
  auxiliary fire service, Cologne,
  1943. HU11712

NORTH-WEST EUROPE

In 1944 the Eastern Front turned increasingly in Russia's favour and in June the Allied invasion of Normandy opened the campaign for the liberation of Western Europe. On 6 June 1944 ('D-Day'), Operation 'Overlord' began, under the American Supreme Commander, General Eisenhower. The assault forces, under the command of General Montgomery, came ashore from some 4,000 landing craft escorted by 600 warships, with air support from more than 10,000 Allied aircraft. Over 156,000 British, Canadian and American troops were landed on the first day, making this the largest combined operation in history. After a month of heavy fighting Caen fell to the British and Canadians. At the end of July American forces broke through the German defences

1   *General Eisenhower, Commander-in-Chief of the Allied Expeditionary Force, addressing American paratroopers on the eve of D-Day.* EA25491

2   *Paratroops of the 1st Airborne Division firing on German positions with a 3-inch mortar, Arnhem, 20 September 1944.* BU1098

3   *Battledress blouse which belonged to Field Marshal Montgomery.*

4   *Commando troops going ashore on D-Day, 6 June 1944.* B5103

I

2

3

4

and advanced rapidly south and east. Paris was liberated on 25 August, Brussels on 3 September. Montgomery's bold plan to open a 'back door' into Germany through Holland ended in failure on 26 September when the British 1st Airborne Division was forced to withdraw after seizing a vital river bridge at Arnhem. A daring German counter-attack in the Ardennes in December was repulsed and in March 1945 Allied troops crossed the Rhine. As agreed at the Yalta Conference in February 1945, the Western Allies halted on the Elbe, allowing the Russians to take Berlin. In the last months of the war, Hitler's mental and physical health deteriorated rapidly and on 30 April he committed suicide in his underground bunker. On 4 May German forces in North-West Europe surrendered to the Commander-in-Chief of the 21st Army Group, Field Marshal Montgomery. The instrument of Germany's unconditional surrender was signed at Eisenhower's headquarters in Rheims on 7 May. Victory in Europe (VE) Day was celebrated the following day.

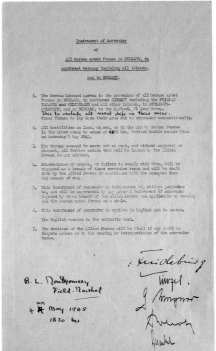

1

1 *The signing of the Instrument of Surrender at 21st Army Group Headquarters on Luneburg Heath, 4 May 1945.* BU5207

2 *The surrender document.* BU5216B

3 *Rocket-firing Typhoons at the Falaise Gap, Normandy 1944. Frank Wootton.*

4 *Sleeve badge of the First Polish Armoured Division*

2

3

4

WAR IN THE FAR EAST

By 1941 Japanese ambitions in Asia and the Pacific had led to a serious deterioration in relations with the United States. On 7 December 1941, without a declaration of war, Japanese carrier-borne aircraft attacked the US Pacific Fleet at its base at Pearl Harbor in the Hawaiian Islands and put most of it out of action. Congress declared war on Japan the next day. The Allies were ill-prepared to defend their possessions in the Far East and by the summer of 1942 the Japanese had overrun the Philippines, Malaya, Burma and the Dutch East Indies. Japan's early successes resulted in the capture of hundreds of thousands of Allied military and civilian personnel, who had to endure malnutrition, disease, forced labour and appalling living conditions. Over a quarter of them died. At Midway in 1942, which like other naval battles in the Pacific was dominated by the aircraft carrier, the Japanese suffered their first major defeat of the war. Soon they were being pushed back throughout their Pacific empire. General MacArthur's forces fought their way through New Guinea to the Philippines; in another series of operations the Solomon Islands were recaptured after savage resistance by the Japanese. In the central Pacific Admiral Nimitz carried out a series of amphibious operations which brought the Americans within bombing range of Tokyo. In the Battle of Imphal-Kohima in 1944 the British Fourteenth Army under General Slim won a decisive victory which removed the Japanese threat to India. By the spring of 1945 the Americans were preparing to invade Japan. President Truman decided to use the newly developed atomic bomb to end the war. Two bombs were dropped – on Hiroshima on 6 August 1945 and on Nagasaki three days later. On 14 August the Japanese surrendered unconditionally.

1

1 *A section of track from the Burma-Siam railway.*

2 *Relics from Hiroshima and Nagasaki.*

3 *Sick prisoner, Changi Gaol, July 1944 Ronald Searle.*

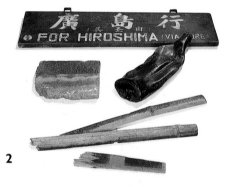

2

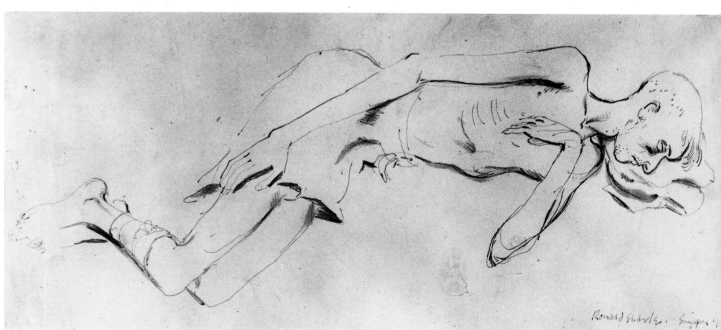

The atomic explosion at Nagasaki, 9 August 1945. MH2629

BELSEN 1945

The exhibition *Belsen 1945* is devoted to the relief effort at the notorious concentration camp after the arrival of British forces in April 1945.

Contemporary film, sound recordings, paintings and photographs, personal mementoes, letters and other documents recall the appalling conditions which existed in the camp and the remarkable operation which succeeded in saving the lives of many of the 45,000 inmates and in rehabilitating the survivors.

2

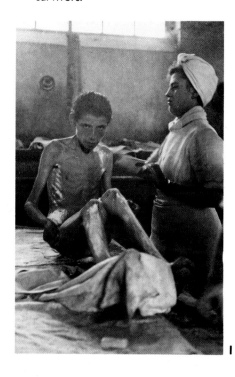

1

1   *An inmate of Belsen receiving care after being evacuated from the camp, May 1945.* BU5473.

2   *A scene inside Belsen camp, 17 April 1945.* BU3811

POST-1945 EXHIBITS

Until new galleries are completed only a small number of exhibits from the post-war era can be displayed. They include a Leopard security vehicle from Rhodesia and a 'Wheelbarrow' remote control bomb disposal vehicle. The Korean War period is represented by a Soviet 122mm field howitzer and the Falklands War by a 21-inch torpedo of the type used by Royal Naval submarines and a Harrier GR3 which was in service with the Royal Air Force.

A British patrol in Korea is briefed, c1952 KOR 603.

VICTORIA CROSS AND GEORGE CROSS

The Victoria Cross and George Cross room houses the Museum's collections of these supreme awards for military and civil gallantry. The centrepiece of the display is the 13-pounder 'Néry' gun and the three VCs won by its crew during the Battle of Mons. The stories of Boy First Class Jack Cornwell, Lieutenant J G Smyth (later Brigadier the Rt Hon Sir John Smyth), Corporal Charles Garforth and other First and Second World War VCs are told. The most recent Victoria Crosses were awarded for bravery during the Falklands War to Colonel 'H' Jones and Sergeant Ian McKay. Among the George Crosses are those won by resistance hero Wing Commander F F Yeo-Thomas, the 'White Rabbit', and by Lieutenant Robert Davies, who saved St Paul's by defusing a bomb which fell close to the cathedral during the Blitz. Related exhibits include a telescope used by Lieutenant Augustus Agar VC and logbooks belonging to Group Captain Leonard Cheshire VC.

The Victoria Cross.

I

1 *Boy First Class Jack Cornwell, VC.* Q27025A

2 *Violette Szabo, GC.* HU16541

3 *Group Captain Leonard Cheshire, VC.* CHI3636

4 *Sergeant Ian McKay, VC.*

2

3

The George Cross.

4

ART GALLERIES

The two suites of galleries on the second floor – each of which comprise an anteroom and three main rooms – are used for the permanent display of works from the Museum's collection of twentieth century art. The First World War paintings are hung thematically. The first room shows the modernist works for which the Museum is best known and the second gallery evokes the 'casualties of war' through the paintings of Sydney Carline, Henry Tonks, Eric Kennington and Stanley Spencer. In the third room, which shows the silence and grief of the immediate end of the war, the key work is Sir George Clausen's *Youth Mourning.* Anna Airy's *A Shop for Machining 15 inch Shells in 1918* and the plaster cast of C S Jagger's *No Man's Land* (1919–1920) are displayed in the anteroom.

1

2

1 *CRW Nevinson*
   French Troops Resting 1916

2 *Paul Nash*
   We are Making a New
   World.

3 *Stanley Spencer*
   Travoys arriving with
   Wounded at a Dressing
   Station at Smol, Macedonia,
   September 1916.

3

Since so much of the art of the
Second World War was in the form
of watercolours, this medium
predominates and is represented by
works by Edward Bawden, Edward
Ardizzone, Anthony Gross, Thomas
Hennell, Edward Burra, Bernard
Meninsky, Edwin la Dell, John Minton,
Henry Moore, John Piper and Graham
Sutherland. Oil painters include
Richard Eurich, Mervyn Peake, Henry
Carr, Evelyn Dunbar, Carel Weight,
William Scott and John Trevelyan.
Meredith Frampton's triple portrait
of Sir Ernest Gowers, Senior Regional
Commissioner for London, and two
of his colleagues is exhibited in the
anteroom to the Second World War
art galleries.

1

2

1   *Meredith Frampton*
      Sir Ernest Gowers, KCB, KBE,
      Lieutenant-Colonel A J Child,
      OBE, MC, and K A L Parker,
      in the ARP Control Room.

2   *Edward Burra*
      Skull in a Landscape.

3   *David Bomberg*
      Bomb Store.

The suite of galleries on the ground
floor includes the John Singer Sargent
Room, which is used for the
permanent display of the famous
painting, *Gassed*, along with five
supporting charcoal studies and
twelve watercolours. *Gassed* was the
largest of a series of paintings
commissioned for a proposed Hall of
Remembrance during the First World
War. The hall was never built but the
Museum has a number of these works
in its collection. The remaining
galleries house temporary exhibitions
drawn from all sections of the
collection, which includes paintings,
prints, posters and sculpture. Details
of temporary exhibitions are available
in the information area in the
entrance hall.

3

HISTORY OF THE MUSEUM

In 1917 the government decided that a National War Museum should be set up to collect and display material relating to the Great War, which was then still being fought. The interest taken by the Dominion governments led to the museum being given the title of Imperial War Museum. It was formally established by Act of Parliament in 1920 and a governing Board of Trustees appointed.

The Museum was opened in the Crystal Palace by King George V on 9 June 1920. From 1924 to 1935 it was housed, under very difficult conditions, in two galleries adjoining the former Imperial Institute, South Kensington.

On 7 July 1936 the Duke of York, shortly to become King George VI, reopened the Museum in its present home. The Museum was closed to the public from September 1940 to November 1946 and vulnerable collections were evacuated to stores outside London. Most of the exhibits survived the war, but a Short seaplane, which had flown at the Battle of Jutland, was shattered when a German bomb fell on the Naval Gallery on 31 January 1941 and some of the naval models were damaged by blast.

At the outset of the Second World War the Museum's terms of reference were enlarged to cover both world wars and they were again extended in 1953 to include all military operations in

which Britain and the Commonwealth have been involved since August 1914.

Apart from a small extension added in the 1960s the galleries remained in their original state until the Museum initiated a major redevelopment scheme in 1986. The first stage of this work, designed by Arup Associates, has been completed and provides the Museum with three times the exhibition space and greatly improved

public facilities. Further developments are planned in stage two of the scheme and will, in due course, give the museum an improved education centre as well as new galleries for permanent and special exhibitions,

1   The Army Section of the Museum at the Crystal Palace in 1920. Q31438.

2   Poster for the IWM by Edward Wadsworth, c. 1936.

3   Bethlem Hospital as it was in 1843 before the building of the dome. MH3478.

including temporary art exhibitions. Work is dependent on government grant and private funding, and donations are vital to enable the scheme to go ahead.

BETHLEM ROYAL HOSPITAL

The building which accommodates the Museum was formerly the central portion of Bethlem Royal Hospital or Bedlam. Designed by James Lewis, it was completed in 1815. Sidney Smirke's dome was added in 1846 and contained the chapel and servants' quarters. The east and west wings were demolished in the early 1930s to make room for the park which now surrounds the museum.

Bethlem Royal Hospital dates back to 1247, when Simon Fitz-Mary, a wealthy alderman and a sheriff of London, founded the Priory of St Mary of Bethlem on the site now occupied by Liverpool Street station. In the fourteenth century the priory began to specialise in the care of the insane. On the dissolution of the monasteries, Bethlem was seized by Henry VIII. In 1547 the King granted the hospital to the City of London.

Bethlem was moved to a new building in Moorfields in 1676. Until 1770 there were no restrictions on visitors, and the lunatics, who were often manacled or chained to the walls, were a major public attraction.

The hospital was housed in the present building from 1815 to 1930, when it was transferred to Eden Park near Beckenham, Kent.

3

THE MUSEUM'S OUTSTATIONS

HMS *BELFAST*

The cruiser HMS *Belfast* is the last survivor of the Royal Navy's big gun ships and is permanently moored in the River Thames as a floating naval museum.

Launched in 1938, her career began in October 1939 with the seizure of the German merchant vessel *Cap Norte* but soon after she was severely damaged by a mine. Once repaired, HMS *Belfast* took part in the Arctic convoys and played an important role in the Battle of the North Cape on 26 December 1943. On 6 June 1944 the ship was among the first to open fire on the coast of Normandy. The following year she joined the Allied peace-keeping force in the Far East. From 1950 to 1952 HMS *Belfast* provided artillery support for UN forces in the Korean War.

After the ship had finished her active service, the Imperial War Museum initiated efforts to save her from the scrap yard and in 1971 the HMS *Belfast* Trust was formed, which brought the ship to her present berth. In 1978 the Museum assumed full responsibility for the ship. Areas open to the public include the bridge, living quarters, galley, operations room, punishment cells, the engine and boiler rooms, and special naval displays.

For further information telephone 071-407 6434 or write to the Director, HMS *Belfast*, Morgans Lane, Tooley Street, London SE1 2JH.

DUXFORD AIRFIELD

The former Battle of Britain fighter station at Duxford near Cambridge displays over 120 aircraft along with many other exhibits, ranging from armoured fighting vehicles and a giant 9.2 inch coastal gun to midget submarines. Among the aircraft are a RE8 from the First World War and a Junkers Ju52, B-17 Flying Fortress and B-29 Superfortress from the Second World War. Concorde 101 is one of an impressive collection of British civil aircraft which the Duxford Aviation Society has assembled for display at Duxford in association with the Museum.

Visitors may wander through five hangars, three of which date from the First World War. Aircraft can be seen under restoration and, as Duxford's runway is still active, historic aircraft can often be seen taking to the skies. In the summer Duxford has special events and vintage films are shown in a restored 1940s cinema. The original Battle of Britain Operations Room has also been restored. There is an exhibition dedicated to the United States Eighth Air Force, which had a wartime base at Duxford.

For further information telephone Cambridge (0223) 835000 or write to the Director, Duxford Airfield, Cambridge CB2 4QR.

THE CABINET WAR ROOMS

The Cabinet War Rooms comprise the most important surviving part of the underground emergency accommodation which was provided to protect Winston Churchill, the War Cabinet and the Chiefs of Staff of Britain's armed forces against air attack during the Second World War. The rooms, which lie some three metres below ground level in the basement of the Government Offices, Great George Street, became operational a week before Britain declared war on Germany and remained in use until the surrender of Japan in August 1945. In 1981 the Property Services Agency of the Department of the Environment invited the Imperial War Museum to advise on the historical aspects of the rooms' restoration and to manage

HMS Belfast at her moorings opposite the Tower of London.

Aerial view of Duxford.

The Central Map Room, Cabinet War Rooms.

them after they were opened to the public in 1984. On 1 April 1989 the Trustees of the Museum accepted formal responsibility for the administration of the site and its contents.

Today visitors can view a complex of twenty-one rooms, including the Cabinet Room, the Map Room – where information from all fronts was collected – and the Prime Minister's Room, which Churchill used to make a number of his wartime broadcasts.

For further information telephone 071-930 6961 or write to the Curator, Cabinet War Rooms, Clive Steps, King Charles Street, London SW1A 2AQ.

THE REFERENCE DEPARTMENTS

Besides the material displayed in the public galleries, which has already been described, the Museum's reference departments hold extensive collections. These are available to the public. In all cases it is essential to make an appointment either by telephone or by letter to the Keeper of the relevant department.

DEPARTMENT OF DOCUMENTS

The Department of Documents is a repository for documentary records of all types relating to warfare in the twentieth century. The collection falls into two main groups, one consisting of British private papers and the other mainly of captured German material.

The Department holds one of the largest collections in this country of personal papers of British citizens. Senior officers' records, notably those of Field Marshal Viscount Montgomery of Alamein, provide valuable information about particular commands and campaigns during the two world wars. The personal diaries, letters and unpublished memoirs of servicemen and civilians who did not rise to high positions form a rich source of evidence for the social as well as the military historian. The Department's collections include manuscript material of the war poets Isaac Rosenberg and Siegfried Sassoon. The Department administers several important groups of German documents relating to the period 1920 to 1945 and is the national repository of the records of the trials of the major German and Japanese war criminals after the 1939–1945 war.

DEPARTMENT OF EXHIBITS AND FIREARMS

The Department of Exhibits and Firearms is responsible for the acquisition, cataloguing and storage of the Museum's three-dimensional objects, such as uniforms, badges, medals, edged weapons, models, aircraft, boats, artillery and military vehicles. It also administers the national collection of modern firearms, which includes examples of almost all weapons issued on a significant scale by the major powers in the two world wars and representative examples illustrating the development of firearms from the nineteenth century to the present day. Many more notable exhibits in the collections may be seen in the galleries and there are extensive reserve collections.

DEPARTMENT OF PRINTED BOOKS

The Department of Printed Books is a reference library holding over 100,000 books and 25,000 pamphlets, 15,000 volumes of periodicals, and 15,000 maps and technical drawings. While the strength of the collection lies in its detailed coverage of all aspects of the two world wars, there are also extensive holdings relating to more limited conflicts of the twentieth century.

The outstanding collection of British, French, German and American unit histories includes the main published histories of armies down to battalion level, of navies down to individual ships and of air forces down to squadrons. There is an important collection of technical manuals and handbooks. The pamphlet collection has numerous examples of wartime propaganda, ration books, enlistment cards, army forms and other ephemera. There are news cuttings and handouts from the files of the Ministry of Information, and transcripts of the BBC monitoring reports from September 1939.

Four hundred and fifty professional and specialist journals are currently taken. There is also a collection of many service and civilian periodicals which were produced for a limited period.

The map collection is particularly extensive for the First World War and includes trench maps, and situation and order of battle maps.

DEPARTMENT OF ART

The Department of Art is responsible for the Museum's collection of paintings, drawings, sculptures and prints, numbering over 12,000 works, and for its collection of posters, medallions and printed ephemera. The Department also holds a virtually complete archive relating to the British official war artist schemes of the two world wars.

The fine-art collection dates predominantly from 1916 when Muirhead Bone was sent out to the Western Front as the first official war artist.

The collection of over 50,000 posters is fully international in scope and includes posters dating from 1914 to the present day.

In the post-war era the Museum has continued to enlarge and improve its collections of art through gifts and purchase. Recent acquisitions of contemporary art have reflected present attitudes to the First and Second World Wars as well as to the threat of nuclear war. In addition the Aristic Records Committee, formed in 1972, continues the tradition of the War Artists Advisory Committee by commissioning artists to record activities of the British forces today.

DEPARTMENT OF SOUND RECORDS

The Department of Sound Records is a comprehensive archive, housing over 12,000 hours of historical recordings.

Through the department's oral history programme, members of staff interview men and women from all walks of life about their wartime experiences. Non-military aspects of war and the experiences of non-combatants are as important as the specifics of life in the battle zones.

As well as soliciting interviews the Department collects relevant recordings from radio and television organisations. The Department also holds recordings of lectures given at the Royal United Services Institute for Defence Studies; and a collection of sound effects associated with war. Recordings are deposited in the archives by the British Council, the British Forces Broadcasting Service, the Central Office of Information, Deutsches Rundfunkarchiv and the US National Archives. Donations from private individuals are also received.

DEPARTMENT OF FILM

The Department of Film's collection originated with the official films shot by British cameramen during the First World War. The films, from all theatres of the war, were of military, naval and air operations together with material dealing with the home front.

The Second World War saw a vast expansion of the Museum's holdings, much of it in the form of unique unedited record film of land, sea and air operations. Edited Second World War British holdings range from Ministry of Information shorts and official newsreels to full length features and documentaries.

The Department is concerned in a more general way with all film relating to war and its political and social causes and effects. It has a notable collection of German documentary and feature films as well as extensive holdings of Nazi newsreels. Other foreign collections include Indian newsreels, a partial set of Soviet newsreels from 1941 to 1944, the American propaganda series *Why We Fight* and smaller Japanese and Italian collections.

The Department continues to collect post-Second World War film, including not only official material from government departments but also major television series.

DEPARTMENT OF PHOTOGRAPHS

The Department of Photographs is a national archive of over five million prints and negatives dealing with warfare in the twentieth century. Its collection is mainly concerned with the two world wars but also includes material on other conflicts involving Britain and the Commonwealth. The foundations of the collection were laid by the official photographers of the First World War who, from 1916 onwards, were employed in every theatre of war and on the home front. The collection was augmented by material from the Dominions, America, Germany and other countries involved.

During the Second World War the Ministry of Information supervised a greatly extended scheme of official photography and passed the accumulated records to the Museum for preservation. Since the Second World War the Department has continued to receive official military photographs. The bulk of the collection is black and white though since 1943 a certain amount of colour material has been received.

The Department is actively engaged in expanding its collection and is interested in the work of both professional and amateur photographers.

The reading room used by visitors to the Departments of Printed Books and Documents is housed in the dome of the building, originally designed as the chapel for Bethlem Hospital.

Winston Churchill, photographed by Cecil Beaton.

Prussian General Officer's pickelhaube, c.1911.

GENERAL INFORMATION

MAIL ORDER

Museum publications including books, videos, postcards and facsimile documents, along with a selection of gifts and souvenirs, may be ordered by post. Write to the Business Development Officer for a free illustrated mail order catalogue.

MAILING LIST

If you would like to be added to our mailing list for regular information send your name and address to the Marketing and Trading Office.

FRIENDS OF THE IMPERIAL WAR MUSEUM

Join the Friends of the Imperial War Museum and enjoy benefits including free entry to the Museum and its outstations. Membership details from the Friends Office 071-416 5255.

EDUCATION SERVICE

The Museum's education service offers schools and colleges a wide range of activities to support work on twentieth century history and literature. The service concentrates mainly on the social impact of the two world wars.

For further information please write to the Education Officer. Schools can be added to the education mailing list free of charge.

RECORDED INFORMATION AND GENERAL ENQUIRIES

For up-to-date programmes of films, talks and exhibitions ring 071-820 1683. The number for all other enquiries is 071-416 5000.

HIRE OF THE MUSEUM

The Large Exhibits Gallery and the Board Room may be hired for receptions of all kinds. Further information from the Marketing and Trading Office.

IMPERIAL WAR MUSEUM TRUST

The Museum welcomes donations from members of the public wishing to support its work, including the improvements planned for stage two of its development scheme. The Trust is registered with the Charity Commissioners under the number L244774/2.

Address for all correspondence: Imperial War Museum, Lambeth Road, London SE1 6HZ.

Published by the Imperial War Museum, Lambeth Road, London SE1 6HZ.
© The Trustees of the Imperial War Museum 1989. Revised 1990, 1992.
ISBN 0 901627 50X

Designed by Peter Dolton.
Design and production in association with Book Production Consultants plc, 25–27 High Street, Chesterton, Cambridge CB4 1ND.

Photography of new museum galleries by Reeve Photography, Cambridge and Imperial War Museum.
Film origination by Anglia Graphics, Bedford.
Printed and bound in England by George Over Ltd., Rugby.